Soul Survivor

Vol. 2 : The Rising Son

B. Poe

Soul Survivor Vol. 2: The Rising Son
Copyright © 2020 by LightWorx Publishing, LLC

ISBN 978-0-578-77668-2

Printed in the United States of America

Published in paperback in 2020 by LightWorx Publishing

<u>Cover Photo & Art</u> - **Copyright©2020 by LightWorx Publishing**

<u>Cover Concept</u> - **Fabrice Malette**

<u>Graphic Illustration</u>- **J ASH B DESIGNS**

Contents

Chapter 1: The Stargazer

Chapter 2: Spirit's Scribe

Chapter 3: Revolutionary

Chapter 4: Love's Conquest

Chapter 5: Reflections

Chapter 6: Free Range

Chapter 7: Scorpio Saga

This work is dedicated to these words:

"I AM"

Chapter 1:
The Stargazer

"The events on Earth are governed by the movements of the heavenly bodies"

-Mark Booth

Experience

Clouds in the sky among the night
Flashes
They say light years away
Off in the distance
Drawing from your energy
While crickets play their symphony
Vibes and sounds that drop hints for
Jumping into electronic memo pad
May soon need a socket
My Soul's batteries run
Longer than Life
Matter of fact
Eternally
Moving like the symbol
On Recycle bins
No fear no sin
Experiences from the most delirious
To somewhat serious
Laughing hard without the buffoonery
This is not new to me
Experience all glued to me

The Lightning

The Lightning's doing its thing
In its dance unfazed
'Cause we run high
With that energy
Call it synergy
Untamed
No liturgy
A land where actions speak
Louder than words
Eyes all seeing
Real live scripture
The picture -in- picture
Dream within a dream
Lights in the sky scene
Put balance in a triple beam scheme
With Trinity themes
It's not death as it seems
Sipping Noni we clean

Liquid Dreams

Liquid Dreams
Liquid Rhythms
Liquid Flows
For the solar spots that blow
Integrations of the dark and light
Characterized as eclipse
Melanin now dines on eternal sunshine
DNA re- patterned
Source's Plan B blueprints
De-activate the bad mon chips
Previous words spoken synthesized
We're now breathing Abrahamic close to Infinite minds
TV dramas turn to reality
Parallel views of the Milky Way Galaxy
There's a quotient for this moment
Where metaphysics and substance is greater than
Vanity

Focus Flows

Glaring at the moon
Focus Flows between brows
Revving up Third eye
A secondary figure reflects
Pale in human illusionary color
Sights into other dimensions
We can see what's next
As we make our Ascension
Precognition
Waiting on Yah's direction
If no justice
Then no peace
A full-fledged
Insurrection
For centuries of rejection
Because of this strong complexion

Wormwood

Imprints of the trees
Covered by blinds by design
We're Divine
So I see through foliage
A mixture of green and fire
My desire to be loved up
Head gone like a riddim
I'm in 'em like venom
Inside Bruce Lee denims
Asiatic acrobatic
In my thoughts
Took a leap from Mars without scars
How we stand below stars
Source's order
The gavel came down
We live long instead of shorter

Lions Gate

It's 8/8
On The *Lion's Gate*
Downloads trying to penetrate
Light codes want to infiltrate
This upgrade is more than essential
New motherboard in the house
Taking up residential
Embracing more of that Nano
Form an alliance with science
Put together stems with a cell
All we need is a shell
Advancements coming in droves
These things just can't be for sale

Chapter 2:
Spirit's Scribe

"One of the hardest things in life is having words in your heart that you can't utter"

-James Earl Jones

Sleuth

The religion I subscribe to
Is truth
Whether on paper
Or in a booth
I'm *Sleuth*
Researching and searching keywords
Implanted on the mind
By Angel or Guide
To Heaven letters
I subscribed
Jah as the Messenger
Spirit as the Scribe
Words come alive

Connect

Lasik vision precision
Ill vantage point
We anoint the joints
Analyze the points
Sometimes
Sip elixir
They say the leaves were for the
Healing of the nations
Clear as day with light rays
The electricity in our temples
Wired not so simple
Things indeed were all so simple
From an innocent mind's perspective
Reflective on nostalgia's algebra
Deeper memories link with the present
Living now to *Connect* the dots later
Towards the center
The DJ moves the fader

Regressions

School daze
Lucid gaze
Clock strikes 11
A sphinx and pyramid
Appeared on paper
Apparently I as artist
In hindsight looked back
To moments of past- life *Regressions*
Without the need for a session
Rising in the use of my mind's facilities
Momentum with agility
Ability to legitimately
Do as we please with ease
Tried and true alliteration
Got an A for following
A weird temptation
Filing chapters away
Feelings pure with elation
When Spirit came to say
That we grew today

Higher Order

I heard the Seraphim playing their harps
Luminated 8
Piano C sharps
Keep armor for the cosmic ocean sharks
Their teeth sink to rip souls
From their hearts
Dark dimension beings
Peeking through holes to grab a hold
In our dismay we shoo 'em away
As we know today's not the day
To dance with the devil
On that lower self-level
Sweet serpentine
Ascends the spine
Coil malleable like foil
Coccyx rocket
Chakra elevation music
A spiral symphony from
Downtown to the crown
It's imperative to feel
Not only hear the sounds

Legacy

Inspiration from the graveyards
A calico cat blends in
With the leaves and jumps off railings
For the edge
Seen me on the ledge
Made a pledge before council
To bring forth the Light
To make things on Gaia right
Pain will be your plight
But glory the world's story
Transformer
Garvey to Sojourner
Divine Masculine to Feminine
Yeah them again
Truth fighters holding lighters
For those who thought they were outsiders
Charlot to Chatelain they government names
Yet carry the *Legacy*
Hands emerge from soil with
Papyrus messages
My sixth sense can't take them all in
While I stand above the physical
Of my Matriarchs
Vintage papers I picked up stating
The common thread on these grounds is
Love

Celebrate

Last night I heard the Angels
Knocking at my windows
Wanting to convene and *Celebrate*
Walking with me through my toil
Now victories galore
Ceiling to the endless floor
I had to fall down to Earth
To understand what it is that's glory
Looked in the mirror
Exposed my wings
Heard them chant
I heard them sing
Taps on the windows moved like
Beats per minute
The chorus was clear
We're all in it infinite

Shadow

Did the *Shadow* work
Praised hell
Then came back to me
It's all Nirvana
Heaven
The Inner Alchemy
Unlocked the Seals
Kept it real
So they came after me
144
At your door
We don't speak blasphemy
New York Nephilim
New Jeru
Black Knights
Backing me
In ATL
I lay my dome
Smoke off the balcony

Chapter 3:
Revolutionary

"Freedom is not something that one people can bestow on another as a gift. Thy claim it as their own and none can keep it from them"

-Kwame Nkrumah

The 33rd

The battle was fought
On *The 33rd*
Dogon so we lick wounds to come home soon
After the monsoon
Tree branches on asphalt
Melted snow flows down the river
Seasons change when faces turn North
No longer shivers
Capstone to headstone I'm headstrong
From adjacent views
Of our common rites of passage
Apartments and tenements
Where we used to hop over flights of stairs
Only to climb up Jacob's ladder
Muscles fatter by design
Spiral staircase to the Divine
The day started cloudy
We're now closer to Sunshine

Elohim

Warrior pose for a black belt's
Forward leaning stance
We do the Mandingo dance
Chanting "Fire!" "Fire!"
Women beat breasts
They hold spears
Like Spartans with no fear
We see freedom through
The crystal balls
The fall of vicious empires
Reclaim glory from Amistad stories
Communities fortified
We pledge allegiance
To our forbearance and parents
The griots with wisdom
The shamans of old
The crystal kids with Hearts of Gold
The enemies call us bold
For we won't fold
It was in our destiny to be great
In our destiny to lead
For on our land
The *Elohim* fell
Planted the seed

Soul Bold

Triple 5 *Soul Bold*
Let your soul glow
Release the transatlantic panic
Were we ever frantic?
Kings and Queens
Turn to cultivating pipe cancer
Inna di backyard
Sugar plantation
Haitian
Spells independence
Wars of attrition end
When grounded in Spirit
Bonaparte arts held nothing
As brothers live lavish in Paris
Baby Doc
Martelly rocks
Like a born musician
Parliamentary ink
Fusion for solutions
Bag a Zo's burn without pollution
Just know that when ships dock
Pirates commence the revolution

360 Degrees

Synthetic frills can kill
Vocabulary and memories
Dictionary to Pictionary
Synonyms come soon
We learn holistic balance
To uphold talents
Imhotep scholars scream and holler
360 Degrees
Hippocrates
Falls to his knees
So one can't conceive
Of disease or malaise
In a phase where we
Turn the page and rage
Against the machines
Spend time peeling limes
To extract the bitter
As if it were kosher to reconsider
Work from the heart
The diagnosis is bipolar
When your world falls apart
Proclaim fame with severe dedication
To the arts
One hand provides the parts
The other polishes the full picture
If you seek affirmation
Much is hidden in scripture

Shuck & Jive

They speak on phones from the other side
On their *Shuck and Jive*
The ears ignore what they heareth
'Cause none of it agrees with my Spirit
Dead it before minds can even clear it
A zombie walks medicated in the liver
As if to sear it
Alkaline in the wisdom
To combat the evil spirits
Green Tea trees neutralize the free radicals
Even if emotions yield upset
I understand this sabbatical
It was written before on *White Walls*
Jumper I AM
Hindu memories in Magnus of that
Pretty girl Pam
Thanking Source the information don't drain
Like e-mails with spam

False Flag

Problem- reaction-solution schemes
Maritime
Created over seas
Imagine me falling on bended knee
To *False Flags*
They're cooking up war and fear
My Soul has its sights on a couple of years
Armed with shears
They seek to cut branches from
The Tree of Life
These Angels came to battle with swords
With Leviathan type strikes
Far superior to their knives
Conspiracies so contrived
This message here to save lives

G-Force

Got to run away from corporate
Rise up stronger than a forklift
Can't do another shift
Jumping out the rat race
Its path was more linear
A near even cliff to jump off
As I propel into the sky into the Heavens
Clock on Earth at 11:11
Unflinching towards the Sun
Crystalline in my form
As if we were one
I shine you shine
Moving through dimensions
Back to Source on a course
Garnered by more than *G-Force*
Tank filled with the fire
Angels move when called upon
For prevention
Yes they wonder why I'm always
Talking about this Ascension

Bulletproof

The Brothers got boulevards for going hard
Some got passes by many men Mason
The others on your mixtape or posters
Can't erase them
We all had a dream and knew
The future belonged to those
Who prepared for it today
In the most peaceful and radical
Revolutionary ways
At the end of the day
It was perception that drove down
The road between the Mind and Heart
Taken out with darts
Spirits *Bulletproof*
One smiled
The other aloof
A fruitful hand comes out of pockets
When they come to spread truth

Patterns

Brutality looking more like trauma porn
We shouldn't adorn
I escape with a terpene vape
Like when Maca takes effect
Watch these scenes take shape
Notice patterns
While that man being battered
Choke holds on purpose
Aortic veins being shattered
High tech lynching
While the ops and spectators gather
Officer or Overseer
Etymology so clear
Can't let Corona take root
So may you please hold my beer?
Moving on with no fear
May have to clip up
Hearts so damn sincere

Chapter 4:
Love's Conquest

"Nobody has ever measured, not even poets, how much the heart can hold."

-Zelda Fitzgerald

Brown Sugar

There's a growing rift between my Lover and I
In this shift
Moving from stoked to stoic
Pulling off heroics to save what was once
Fine like wine
Relationships fermented with vapors of Love
A whole new plan
A whole new design
I won't accept refusal nor decline
So long as the sun shine
Every evening rose petals on your pillow
Sweet dreams
Kindness for the weeping willows
Gentle strokes below throws
Warmth of a comforter you once knew
Lay down now *Brown Sugar*
I want to speak to body and produce things for you
By and by baby
Through and through

Lullaby

We had to fall from grace to remember
Our sacred love space
Singing love *Lullabies* in our
Mind's soliloquies
During brief separations
To practice with patience
For when we reconvene for our Love scenes
You and I as pair
Through the years
Make a profound team
Fulfill our dreams
Sewing up seams with the stitches
Hits and misses
Mr. & Mrs.
Hugs and Kisses
Hands on your stamp
Seated at lower spine
As we settle at ease with
Your innate duality
Gemini
Bringing honor to your name as Wife
The most kindred of kin
Let's look forward to our Love story
No longer fighting the wind

The Extremes

I did a back flip from
The initial tastes of her lips
Now somersaults for all my faults
Learning to love
Between *The Extremes*
Tornadoes and hurricanes
Either way
I want her and I
To be grounded in the eye
Of the storm
Holding a hand that's warm
Radiating
To melt her icebox of a heart
Replace me
With where it used to be
So Baby you can see
I'm your Destiny

Original Sins

In a world where whirlwinds spin
To Earth spasms
Babies come from orgasms
Izm's and Schism's
First car geo prizm's
I get'em I got'em I Live'em
I give her
Thrusts to combust
Center of the circle dot spots
With each shot
Closer to Life and Death
Ball games to the movement of the Sun
If victory falls in your corner
It's for you I make this sacrifice
Back to reality
Back to life
Remove the knife
Let the blood shed
All sins forgiven
We move ahead

Down To Mars

It seems as if there is no flame
To be rekindled
I apparently took away her youth
As for me it was my perceived sanity
Although the world crazy
I never give Love lazy
I bet you expect me to accept
Love that is less
Please come step in my Timbs
One day access to all the Love within
Compassion at its finest
My Feminine Highness
A *Down to Mars* girl
In a world filled with greed
Is what a King needs

Damiana Madonna

She holds the sweetest persona
We go hard
Damiana Madonna
Amor Amor
Our beloved designer
Got my eyes like china
Nothing make me feel finer
Inner research behind her
I got the keys to unlock Ezilí
Freedom never forsaken
It's through her eyes we see
At the altar we feed
This sacrifice we bleed
When it comes to front lines
We let you take the lead

The Bird's Bee

The birds don't discriminate
Crows to blue jays
Cherchez a way at bay to
Announce my arrival
Crucified yet survival
Filtering through bibles
So many versions
Thanking God for this excursion
Learning to see truth from fiction
3D depictions
Glimpses of a higher world
Devils fighting the birth of my baby girl
She could be King or Queen
Like we see at the peaks of perimeters
Blue flame buildings stand erect
To create a growing sect
Moving like hen pecks
Procreation
Lips on her neck
Spontaneous bust
Alarm clocks go off
Today we ride the train
Yesterday was a bus

Distractions

We off the rockers
Put motion in these
Magic potions
Potent extravagant scents
Inhaling Natural Mystics
When I kiss lips
Therapeutic ayurvedic
Shilajit from the flea
Oxytocin coasting boasting
Love box contraptions having contractions
Putting in work
Giving her action
For more than satisfaction
Filter out the *Distractions*
While the agents keep tapping

Silent Violence

Felt murdered by your *Silent Violence*
Life's tragedies could be our only
Wakeup call
We spent years traveling
Making strides
Changing roles
One would've thought
We took residency on
Revolutionary Road
Your actions bold
If truth be told
Not completely sold on
What you behold
So if missions could mold
My hand you'll hold
Platinum had its moment
While true purity lies in gold

The Peak

Tonight I won't do much
But it's your soul I'll touch
It's your soul I'll clutch
Let's roll up
The white papers
Skip the Dutch
Tomorrow
We can do brunch
Let me give you a hunch
Where we eat is a treat
Still massaging your feet
Your essence oh so unique
Smile slightly oblique
Girl you know I'm a freak
Got to put you to sleep
We climax to *The Peak*
Off this obelisk

Chapter 5:
Reflections

"The mind will reflect, eyes glazed with a vision of longevity"
-Fabrice Malette

Legion

In the springs of Saratoga
We placed bets
Four legged competition
Angel with a Sword
The longshot position
If I went trifecta
The woman behind the counter
Would've threw up benjamins
My crazy vision
Trying to be exacta
I took a loss
She came up 2nd
Her tattoo landed on my arm
"*Legion* by the Millions"
Were her words
We multiply like allies for the end times
Gabriel knew I'd be a rebel
Sinews fell into palms
Veins popped among arms
Flexing
Wingspans covering the Earth's
Four grid sections

The Seed

So special are the movements
The Seed was planted
I became like an architect
Structuring scenes
With the passion a feign
Would dream to devise his
Latest scheme
Just to get high
The couch I used to write on
Is suddenly missing
I'm suddenly not listening
To another excuse
Unlike him I erect
A home fortified by stones
No loans
Just a stem from a tree of creativity
At a pace of knowing this essence
Holds longevity with levity
As opposed to brevity

Karmic Loop

We gain resolve and fortitude
While running laps on the *Karmic Loop*
The reward
A six pack for completion
A seven for trouble's deletion
An eight seated at the right hand of the great
The nine your fate
At 10 you're straight
Overview on Life
Stories nice to trife
Some roll the dice
So we eat a slice
Pie in the sky
3.14 for the magnum
At your corner store
It's really all
Like a revolving door
Similes and metaphors
For the youths that's hardcore

True Religion

The treasures of the heart and mind
Are *True Religion*
Forward vision
Present moments
Turn style to metro card tokens
Synaptic broken
Chemical burn
Sparks concern
In the backyards of Grayson
Yeah he's a Grey's son
Radiate like the rays sun
Impatient with the connections
After resurrections
Dudes up in my sphere
Now I see it clear
Stand back
The rams back
Fifth element artifact
Thought Love was a heart attack
But we guarding that

Spheres

Moving like planets within a planet
Spheres among *Spheres*
Bioelectric energies
Auras for atmospheres
Tears look like rain
Emotions include pain
Smiles measure for miles
Kilometers for the frowns
When the resonance upside down
Lightning bolts for shock
Like when squares hit the blocks
Our blood precious like diamonds
At 38 we're hot
The hair still 9 ether
If your Soul Loves the Sun
The rays will always seek you

Summer Reading Feedings

Prescriptive literature
Pecola breeds love
While Atticus finch pinch
The syringe holding heroin
Holden Caufield steel
Injection
So catch her in the rye fields
The color purple
Had me in a haze like
Kush and dour hours
Gatsby style
I could go on forever
She said she liked my Strong Island
When we ate at Oyster Bay
Paused to hear Bishop
Preach to Q about the juice
Along the way
Sent flowers to Algernon's funeral
Then fell asleep
Tryptophan effects
The mind eats
Summer Reading Feedings
Knowledge seeps
We can sometimes relate
When it seems the themes takes place
At our front gates

The Paradox

The Paradox is unorthodox
Reefer surfing crazy eyes lazy
I'm wavy on tsunami type waves
Rising no boats for capsizing
As I make my Bermuda triangle at will
Flash through portals
Where time is still or nil
In space I'm an ace
Wasn't meant for one place
IAM that IAM
Here there everywhere
Omnipresent no cares
The people just share
One Love One Heart
Like it was from the start
Separation has no place
When the world falls apart

Seasons

Came into this world between *Seasons*
Fall as my favorite
Falls into the coldest winter
Guaranteed to catch a Nor Easter
Before Easter
Tropical storms are the norm
In the summer
Come with rain
Spring 'been acting funny
Yet more of the same

King's Camera

Sweet Savannah said the
Eyes could be the camera
32 two's what's a brother to do?
Add it up 64
We get Creator numbers
10:10 win win's got you awake from slumbers
Some said "You're on your own brother man"
How's that when we're the world's X Clan?
How's that give a dap to my man
Hand in Hand yeah we moved across the sand
Hieroglyphics get real specific
Psycho-pictographic building structures megalithic
Intrinsic thoughts is what we know that the Universe brought
Extrinsic things is what we thought that the Falsetto sings
We sift through it all with purpose knowing that we are
Kings

Dedicated

It was all done
All in my glory
Thoughts
Happiness to gory
Remain *Dedicated*
Light shining a li'l brighter
At the end of the tunnel
Climbing out this funnel
Life's smorgasbords
We could only take in with swords
Some decline the swine
Yet still feast with the beast
Breaking bread
Rise like yeast
While we watch
What's old and said wonders
Aurora Borealis Solstice lights
Bring on the lighting and the thunder

Chapter 6:
Free Range

"My poetry is cryptic and at times morbid, yet always with a hint of love in it."

-B. Poe

The Drum

Hip Hop be *The Drum*
Spirit be the cadence
Words dance around circles of fire
While we lay in this
MPC to MP3
Pattern masters align thoughts with poetry
Traditional industry act like they be knowing we
They want the words laced with a poverty conscience
So we kick push fiascos for a cause that's more conscious
Tales of Cadmus or Hermes striking the beast
A feeling like the cycle's complete
Brick straws from our feet
Mythical music legends boost
Ascension through these resurrections
Like the alchemist gold
Out of trunks it be sold
Equalized with controls
Kickers put some sound in the pound
From Japan to Yacktown
It's a Sick a Sound
Forming triangular shapes
Bricklayers to mixtapes
B-boys beat box and beat chests
Strong like the apes

Mix - Match

Time to go Gnostic
Under this Bostitch
Number 2 shade
Celtic Nag Hammadi
Mix- Match like
Kilts at the parade
Plaid prints come together
Regardless of weather or whether
We carry weaponry
A shepherd boy sees his peace
Six pence none the richer
They evolve into flippers
With underwater smarts
Not floppers but top shottas
Cutty Sark dark dreams
Translated by Wray and Nephew
We adore the Divine women this season
Something like Heff do

Acoustic Glory

She sung about the mystery of iniquity
Acoustic flow
Problems solved through our history
Full circle ancestry
Keepers of the Earth
Seeds sprout
Without a doubt
To the side we till still
Like a community garden
'Til the brothers are pardoned
Hearts no longer hardened
Inject the sentiments
So it cements
Felt within
God within
Dusting off the books that hold evidence
No longer are they dead
As it was her breathe
That gave us Life
Glory to you Eden
Glory

Ruger

I got a grip upon my hip
Verbal grenade
Up in the stash
My delivery be kosher
While at times
Straight brash
That's math I couldn't even
Choreograph
So why throw out the baby
With the bath water
When Hennessey plays
The war reporter
Word to my daughter
Ruger gets to talking
In this new world order
Threats at perceived borders
Hands on the missile
Love is the pistol
Bullets sink sharp
Something like the Inner Crystals

Solo

On a *Solo* flight
In the dark night
With the bright lights
Where they light lights
Just to get right
In my Dolomites
Or my black Nikes
Uptown Flights
Ol' British Knights
Yeah he down right
For a street fight
Waiting on the signal
It's a green light

Icy

I be buzz light year booting
Hit you Ryu Ayukhen
These dudes be Madden
That's why I be juking
Told my Brethren good lookin'
From out in Crooklyn
Up 87
Yacktown
That's where it's cookin'
Fab Flava
Spicy
Chains shine
No jooks or bookin
So *Icy*
Back on my grind
That's how it's looking

Stereotype

I'm smoking chronic
Listening to Chronixx
Got that skankin sweet
Strands are so bubonic
Rolling down the streets
Off that gin & tonic
Computer Love
Those beats
Auto-tune electronic
Phoenix flows
Like I'm hooked on phonics
Reject the *Stereotypes*
Nothing like Ebonics
Eagle eyes claw feet
Breaking sounds like sonic

Venerable

Catching wrecks with a *Venerable* flex
Expose confederate flags
The symbol
Ausar's X
Jews clues solve
Saturn's Onyx rubix cube
While Zeus smashed Jupiter's daughter
With no lube
Now please follow me
East Coast scoliosis
Shaped like 13 colonies
We took a bath in Florida water
Road the boat upstream to Nova Scotia
All while rocking my Costas
They said how you be knowing
Told them dig deep
'Cause we're supposed to

Respé

On neg tankou'm
Ke'm pap sote
Poske' m konnen
La vie a belle
Peyi mwen
Se pa pou dat
Mwen vin jwen ou
Yo mete'm nan Zin
Yo rele'm Phantom
Poske'm bat
Sou Tabou Combo
Tankou neg Congo
Se nou mem
Ki pi gwo
On Nu Look
Ki pi sho
Men Zenglen
A zam yo
Gen zuti'm
M' pa peur yo
Plen *Respé* pou
Djazz yo

Chapter 7:
Scorpio Saga

"Bad luck for the young poet would be a rich father, an early marriage, an early success or the ability to do anything well."

-Charles Bukowski

Echoes

I am the Lion
Who roars like the *Echoes* of vibrations
Used to bounce off satellites
Blending the ancient with the New
Testaments
We rocking with what Spirit says is relevant
Schools of mystery
Was told would bring misery
When all I'm seeking is to exercise
The God in Me
What was wrong is now proven
To be fallacy
Said they got some words from another galaxy
Found out my anatomy
Takes space within space
Organs fortified
Imitates its shapes

Curse Reversed

Some of the healing has gone reversed
Generational curse
Back with athlete's feet
In these cleats
While I grind the turf
Coffee laced
No hormonal milk
Half pissy smelling blue quilts
But why complain
Derivations of the blue flame
It's more than just the same
Peeps game
Claims blood flowing like crystals underwater
Striking beasts like Sergeant Slaughter
Thoughts of a midnight marauder

Smooth

Kangol quiet signature fixtures
This lead to random lady talk
They don't stalk but
Say things like
"The young in's don't know nothing 'bout that"
Funny thing is my face
Screams youth
My Soul *Smooth* with the old
It won't wrinkle, fold, nor falter
Stronger than the edges of Gibraltar
Mixed with roots and culture
I'm not like them
A respectable man won't assault you
Yet in self defense
I'm both Eagle in Glory while vulture

Back to Zion

Jumped off the cliff
Gravity brought satellites down with me
Clandestine friends fell on their own swords and lies
Fake arrangements for closings
Out of the country were their alibis
Angry but adapt by moving shifty
Rich life yet thrifty
Mind of an entrepreneur and a Moor
Reached 10 years plus one score
We celebrate sipping Barbancourt
Behind closed doors
Give an Ivory Coast toast
Maintain a Kemetic frame of mind
Orion's guarded by Lions
On the Road *Back to Zion*

Signs

Source will send *Signs*
Cardinals to Monarch butterflies
To affirm your rise
No longer hypnotized
Or supervised by cabal
Undercover in a sable
Memories before
Cutting that cord from your navel
Wondering if Cain is Abel
Reality disabled
Tap dance on zero point
Spark a joint
Hop on the 8th Mile
Like I'm in Detroit

Minutiae

They'll sit idly by
Listening and observing
As if they knew the rumblings
Of your Heart and
Did laps in the current it produces
Many eyes Medusa
Caught up in the *Minutiae*
They wonder why I'm reclusive
Hyperbole so exclusive
These people are not inclusive
This is me
Can't act elusive

Psych Ward Solutions

Psychiatric medium security prison
Thanking Source for still living
Greeted by her head bob and wild nods
I can see it through her eyes
She's singing another sad family Love song
Something abusive had gone wrong
Time in a facility limits abilities
So I thought
Starseed Spiritual fast
With every meal I feel drugged up
Spiritual nourishment so one feels Loved up
Body mellow
Minds hearing sounds
Playing the cello
White eye pigmentation effects turn yellow
Unhealthy codeine dreams
Dual hemispheric
I can hear it
Angels walk with us
So why would a Spiritual Warrior fear it

Wordplay

The Angels incarnate
Seem to struggle
On their quest
To find their way home
Caring for others more at times
Than self
The purest of empaths
Feeling auras
From a thousand miles away
What more can I say
Letting the Songs cry
444
Smoke a J
This is God's *Wordplay*

Scorpio Saga

So much pain and glory
In one page stories
Scorpio Sagas
The collective man or woman
Jam packed with the power
Of the full zodiac
Equipped with a stinger
Dead man's ringer
Rebirth on Earth
Red white or black shells
Intuition swells
To exponential proportions
Switch up of personalities
Friendly extortions
A keen sense of my sphere allows man
To approach men with caution
Loving all trusting a few
While doing your best
To be detrimental to none
Shakespearean philosophies
Born under the Sun
Six days into the eleventh month
In eighty one
A Supernova formed in the Earth's
Outskirts and fell as one

Inner Mastery

Life path of a 9
No walk on easy street
You see
We used to walk the beat
Singing the ill street blues
Now we laced up and walk in
Inner Mastery shoes
All knowledge being born
Become conjoined with cipher
So we can decipher
How Spirit runs through veins
Like blood in our every fiber
Relaying as transcriber
These fingers moving the pen
Life's poetry is the driver
We wonder 'til we relate
I AM
Soul Survivor

About the Author

B. Poe was born and raised in the Village of Nyack, located on the lower Hudson River valley right outside of New York City. He currently resides in Atlanta, GA with his family. He is a graduate of Albany State University in Albany, N.Y. with a B.S. in Business Administration and B.A. in the Africana studies. He continued his educational pursuits and attained an MBA in Entrepreneurship with the Keller Graduate School of Management. He is the Son of Haitian roots that spread seeds in the United States and most importantly a Son of God. There is a time where one receives their calling in life and B. Poe found a portion of his purpose through writing during a period of Rebirth where the affirmation of Creator, God, Almighty, Jehovah, Yahweh, Allah, and All-That-There-Is....came from within.

"I never ask you to conform but to only listen and in the distance a Light shall glisten"

-B.Poe